Curious
KENTISH
TOWN

Curious

KENTISH
TOWN

Martin Plaut and Andrew Whitehead

FIVE LEAVES PUBLICATIONS

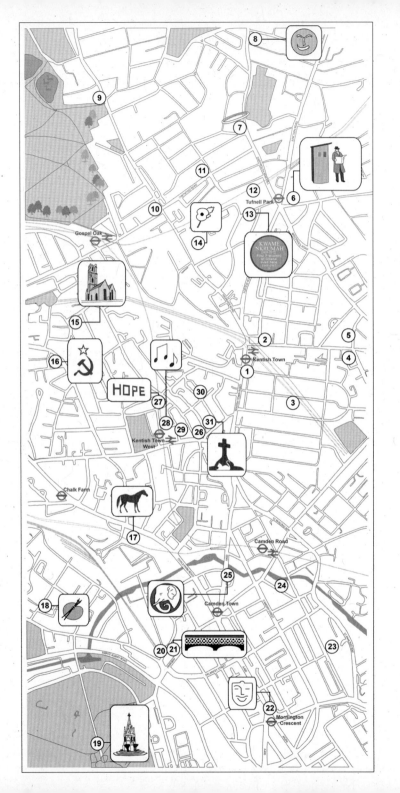

CONTENTS

INTRODUCTION

Kentish Town is a fascinating, diverse and historic area – full of interesting nooks and crannies that have developed over the years. In this book we have delved into some of them.

We only imposed two selection criteria for the places we wrote about: that they should be within twenty minutes walk of Kentish Town tube station and that they should interest us. So some – like Mornington Crescent tube station and the Primrose Hill Studios – are not in Kentish Town at all. For this we make no apology.

Our choice was eclectic and probably eccentric. Some readers will feel that some of our selection should have been excluded; others that we have left obvious candidates out. How did we fail to include Gove Cottage, the house that Lord Horatio Nelson would often stay in with his uncle, William Suckling, next to the Castle Inn, then backing onto the river Fleet? Or the Kentish Town Goods Yard, from which four circus elephants escaped in 1884, knocking their keeper to the ground and careering round the neighbourhood until they were finally cornered in Pemberton Terrace? We ask the reader's indulgence for these and any other misdemeanours.

Between us we have lived in this neck of north London for more than fifty years, yet we learnt a good deal through our research. We hope you enjoy what we found!

1 | DUST-UP IN ISLIP STREET

What an unsettling piece of political theatre! Several thousand fascists lined-up in a Kentish Town side street, with bugles, banners and a would-be supremo, surrounded by a much larger crowd determined to give them a hard time. The leader-in-waiting was Oswald Mosley. The marchers were supporters of the British Union of Fascists. And the date was Sunday, 4 July 1937 – a couple of years before the outbreak of the Second World War.

And the place? Sleepy Islip Street off Kentish Town Road, close to the tube and overground station. Not the likeliest of venues. The press photo shows Mosley – he's the one in the light suit and dark shirt, flanked by dark suited colleagues, in front of the fascist standard – leading his supporters along the street to Kentish Town Road and on to a rally at Trafalgar Square.

There was a history of extreme right-wing organisation in Kentish Town through the 1930s. The BUF and the still more hard-line Imperial Fascist League organised meetings here – and met lively opposition, with fights, arrests and injuries. But this wasn't the fascists' main London stronghold – that was in and around Bethnal Green, adjoining fiercely anti-fascist areas such as Stepney with its large Jewish population.

The Battle of Cable Street in October 1936 was a huge setback for Mosley's movement. Mass protests in the East End forced the fascists to abandon plans to march through the area. The following summer the BUF tried to regroup by again marching through the East End. The government invoked the newly passed Public Order Act to ban any procession through mainly Jewish areas, and so Mosley instead turned his gaze to our part of town.

The local Labour Party was furious and demanded that the Home Secretary keep the fascists out of Kentish Town as much as the East End. 'Islip Street,' they complained, is 'a narrow working-class street previously unused, and quite unsuitable for political demonstration'. But the march was allowed to go ahead.

'Although there were probably 6,000 marchers assembled in Islip Street,' *The Times* reported, 'their numbers were dwarfed by the crowd which collected in the locality.'

'When Sir Oswald Mosley arrived he was greeted with the fascist salute and cries of "Hail Mosley" from the Fascist ranks,' said the

Glasgow Herald, 'while a large section of the crowd began to sing the "Internationale" . . . Sir Oswald, his hand raised in salute, moved off at the head of one of the sections. A portion of the crowd, which had run on ahead of the procession, attempted to stop it by forming a human barrier 10 to 12 deep across the roadway. Mounted police rode into the crowd, and after a brief resistance the barrier gave way.'

Ten anti-fascist demonstrators were arrested in Kentish Town, charged mainly with insulting words and behaviour. One of them had, said the police, clenched his fist in the air as the procession moved off and shouted: 'Come on boys, we'll stop the ——s.' When arrested he insisted: 'I came here to help my gentile friends. They help us.'

The Mosleyites managed to get to Trafalgar Square and stage their rally – which they sought to portray as a victory over 'red terror'. But they were surrounded by a much bigger crowd of anti-fascists.

The BUF never had a single councillor elected anywhere in London. Mosley, along with many of his most active supporters, was interned during the war and afterwards he lived mainly abroad.

2 | 'HEY HO, COOK AND ROWE'

A plaque on the wall of Kennistoun House on Leighton Road reads: 'In memory of Don Cook and the Rent Battles of 1959–1964'. It's not a blue plaque, nor indeed the handiwork of the council, but a tribute to one of north London's most tenacious campaigners on behalf of council tenants. This was the setting of his biggest battle with the authorities.

In the mid-1950s, St Pancras Borough Council was a by-word for municipal radicalism, and famously flew the red flag from the town hall on May Day. That came to an abrupt end when the Conservatives won the 1959 council elections: 'Council Rents Up, Red Flag Down, Closed Shop Out' was the headline in the *North London Press*.

The rent rises were resisted by a borough-wide tenants' movement largely led by Communists such as Don Cook and Labour left-wingers. In January 1960, more than a thousand St Pancras tenants staged a partial rent strike, paying only the old amount. The council issued hundreds of eviction notices, and by the summer – partly because of falling support and partly a tactical decision – only a handful were still on rent strike, notably the two 'rent rebels', Don Cook, an engineer at an aircraft factory, and Arthur Rowe, a waiter.

At the end of August, both men barricaded themselves into their flats – Don Cook at the top floor of Kennistoun House, and Arthur Rowe at Silverdale House on Hampstead Road. The issue caught national attention. On Leighton Road, Cook and his supporters used old pianos, doors and barbed wire to fortify the flat, and even placed an iron bedstead on the roof. Cook is uppermost of the two men featured in this wonderfully dramatic image from a Pathé news reel.

Edie Cook, Don's wife, stayed at a friend's flat on the floor below, ready to sound a ship's bell to mobilize support if the bailiffs approached. At first light on 22 September 1960, the bell sounded – hundreds of police had sealed off the area and the evictions were underway.

At Hampstead Road, Arthur Rowe was winkled out after the bailiffs smashed a hole in a brick wall. The battle at Kennistoun House was more keenly contested. 'Four bailiffs escorted by police raced up the stairs to Mr Cook's flat,' reported *The Times*, 'but were kept at bay for nearly 30 minutes. Oil was thrown at them, they were struck at with

sticks and one bailiff received a head wound when he was hit by a fish tank.'

The bailiffs eventually forced they way in through the ceiling of a back bedroom. They found Don Cook and a friend having a cup of tea at the kitchen table.

The forced evictions galvanised the tenants and their supporters. That evening thousands marched on St Pancras town hall and faced police apparently keen to get their own back for the indignities they had faced that morning. 'Truncheons Out in St Pancras', was the headline in *The Times*. Dozens of protesters were hurt and scores arrested. A news reel entitled 'Eviction Battle On!' – you can find it on YouTube – said of the clashes: 'There has been nothing in London on this scale since the hunger marches of nearly thirty years ago.'

The following day the government took the rare step of invoking the Public Order Act to ban all demonstration in St Pancras for three months.

Don Cook and Arthur Rowe captured the attention of the renowned folk singer Peggy Seeger, who wrote and recorded (with her partner, the equally great Ewan MacColl) 'Hey, Ho, Cook and Rowe':

> *Hey, ho, tell them no*
> *With a barb-wire fence and a piano,*
> *Took a thousand cops to make them go,*
> *Three cheers for Cook and Rowe!*

It's not the world's greatest protest song, but hey (ho), it's by Peggy Seeger and it's about a Kentish Town rent strike – and that's not bad!

And what happened next? Labour swept back to power at St Pancras in 1962 on a promise to rescind the rent rises . . . but never fully delivered. So the rent battles carried on, but not quite with the same ferocity.

3 | THE CAVERSHAM ROAD *SHUL*

Mention to even devout local Jews the Kentish Town synagogue, and you are likely to get a bemused look. But there was one – built for the purpose, used for worship for seventy years, and still standing. Where? On Caversham Road, alongside the rail lines. The sort of building you can walk past hundreds of times and barely notice, but well worth a closer look.

The North West London Synagogue was established in 1890 in leased rooms on York Way. Ten years later, it moved into purpose-built premises – the land was bought from the Midland Railway – on Caversham Road, just five minutes walk from Kentish Town's high street.

The building was distinctly more modest than many north London synagogues – single storey, with room for 200 or so worshippers. The 'new building has no pretence to architectural beauty', the *Jewish Chronicle* declared rather harshly. The drawing it published, reproduced here, suggests a neat, simple structure – with four small corner pinnacles each bearing a Star of David, and an eye-catching square glass dome with larger Star of David aloft.

The opening merited a two-page report in the *Jewish Chronicle*, and the Chief Rabbi spoke at the consecration – though not entirely comfortably. 'It must be admitted, I fear,' he declared 'that hitherto the Jewish residents of Camden Town have evinced but scant interest in public worship.' There were at that time at least fifteen Jewish shops and businesses on Kentish Town Road (fruiterers, confectioners, oilmen, tobacconists, tailors, hairdressers) – probably the nucleus of a congregation which measured a respectable 152 at the religious census conducted over Passover/Easter 1903.

Over the years, attendance diminished. Peter Renton in his book *The Lost Synagogues of London*, records that 'the congregation consisted mainly of shopkeepers who came early to Sabbath prayers, then

returned to their business, occasionally having to be dragged back to keep the quorum going.'

By the early 1970s, the congregation had all but gone and the synagogue fell into disuse. A combination of vandalism and neglect saw the building reduced to what the *Jewish Chronicle* described as 'a dripping, roofless, rot-infested wreck with everything of Jewish interest smashed or removed.'

A saviour came in the form of architects who designed, among other things, synagogues. They restored the building for use as their offices, took down the now unsalvageable dome, and built what designers would call a mansard roof, allowing both more space and lots of light.

There's nothing about the building today which reveals its origins as a synagogue, though aspects of the initial design, particularly the curving brickwork above some of the windows, are still evident. It's 69 Caversham Road if you are curious, now the light, spacious and well-appointed office of a concert management company, and when we popped in to see if they knew about the building's history, yes they did.

And the nearest synagogue these days? Well, the few worshippers who saw out the last days of the Caversham Road *shul* transferred to the Highgate Synagogue on Archway Road which has since relocated to just north of Highgate village.

4 | A COUNTRY COTTAGE

If you are looking for a rustic idyll among the bustle and grime of north London, then take a stroll down Torriano Cottages. That architectural sage Nikolaus Pevsner gave the houses his benediction: 'an unexpectedly rural cul-de-sac of Victorian cottages'. Actually, it's not a dead end at all, but a narrow, hidden away, unadopted street zigzagging from Leighton Road to Torriano Avenue, which entices above all because it's not what you expect in dear old Kentish Town.

Most of the older houses are mid- or late-Victorian, small and simple, but with an ample dose of charm – and gardens much larger than you might expect. The hand painted street signs, the gas lamps, and the abundant foliage all add to the aura. Once a refuge for the lower middle class and skilled working class, this is now largely a community

of architects, writers and media types. And once they have settled in Torriano Cottages, they take root.

Back in the day, Joshua Prole Torriano (how did he get that name?) inherited, through his wife it seems, several fields which stretched from the current site of Kentish Town station all the way to the other end of what is now Leighton Road. When the estate was developed from the mid-nineteenth century, a cluster of developments took the Torriano name. Well, it does have a certain ring to it.

What seem to be the first of the cottages were advertised for auction in *The Times* in the spring of 1847 – 'two well-built villas . . . commanding delightful views of Highgate, Hampstead, Harrow, and the surrounding country'. Once you strip away the estate agent-style flourishes – yes, even then! – you're left with a couple of fairly modest two-up, two-downs.

The 1851 census lists just two Torriano Cottages – the best bet, say the architects among the current residents, is that these are what are now numbered 4 and 5. By 1871, there were eleven occupied cottages – with more than half the households headed by clerks of various descriptions. By 1911, there was quite a showing of police constables (four in all) and workers on the railways (two porters, a guard, an inspector and a signalman) – and even though all the houses were small, most were home to more than one family, and in all a hundred people were crammed in to thirteen properties.

The heart of the Cottages is a terrace of seven houses, built bit-by-bit but all in essence two storey. Across the way, there are even more intriguing buildings, notably the splendid Davis (initially Davies) Cottage. Its current occupant believes the house is late Georgian and may originally have been a farm. That's open to question. What can be retrieved of the initial design (and again, it was built as two-up and two-down) has a lot in common with numbers 1 and 2 – which are probably of mid-Victorian vintage.

Whenever the cottage was built, it's a treasure – there are not many detached houses in NW5 with such impressive design. The spacious garden includes a pond featuring a mill stone retrieved from nearby undergrowth 'It's amazing, *rus in urbe*,' declares its resident for the past twenty years. 'You wake up and hear nothing but bird song.' That at least compensates for going to sleep amid the not always decorous noises from the a-bit-too-nearby Torriano pub.

Not that time has stood still in Torriano Cottages. This is a low rise, but high density, locality – with modern infill both on the back gardens of houses facing Leighton Road and on the site of what was a joiner's yard. So much so, the house numbers now extend to 33 Torriano Cottages. Yet somehow, the spot has managed to safeguard its tranquillity in spite of the squeeze of modern development.

Among the latter day properties is a house designed by Philip Pank fifty years ago as his own home which attracted Pevsner's eye even more than the Victoriana – 'an unassuming family house on a tiny site, one-storeyed, delicately detailed and landscaped, with a roof garden and a tree rising from an internal courtyard'. If you want to have a gander, and you should, it's number 15.

5 | THE POETS' MEETING HOUSE

Of all the nooks and crannies in Kentish Town, the locality around the junction of Torriano Avenue and Leighton Road is among the most intriguing. There's the serendipity of the splendidly named Charlton King's Road – the hidden away Torriano Mews – the already discussed near arcadian delight of Torriano Cottages. And at 99 Torriano Avenue, easily overlooked as it does little to proclaim its public purpose, the Torriano Meeting House has for thirty years been a cherished centre for participatory arts of a generally radical bent.

In all sorts of ways, the Meeting House feels like a throwback – an entirely admirable echo of a bygone era. There's the building's appearance – commercial premises at one time, though with the lower half of the display windows long since boarded up. A century ago, 99 Torriano Avenue was a hairdresser's. During the Second World War, the building was – Susan Johns, who runs the centre, has heard say, though with what authority she's not sure – a café or restaurant.

Now, the bare floor boards, the steps up to a raised platform, the vintage stackable chairs, the formless couch, the embroidered room divides, the upright piano dating from 1902 (a Collard & Collard, so almost certainly made in Camden), lend a retro aspect to the surroundings. Reinforced by the use to which the space is sometimes put.

The Unity Folk Club meets here every month – an institution which has its roots way back in the left-wing Unity Theatre, and initially gathered in the theatre bar (not all that far away, on Goldington Street on the northern edge of Somers Town) before that building burned down in 1975. It is democratic to its core – going round in a circle until everyone who wants to has had a chance to sing or play or read. The evening we called in, twenty-five or so enthusiasts were there, most elderly and spritely, singing in Serbo-Croat and Zulu as well as offering renditions of 'The Ballad of Joe Hill', a couple of Ewan MacColl songs and an anthem for the Occupy movement, and playing instruments from mandolin to dulcimer.

But it's the Torriano poets who have made the Meeting House's reputation – and the Hearing Eye poetry press is also based here. Both are associated with John Rety, a Hungarian-born visionary described in his 2010 obituary in the *Daily Telegraph* as 'a chess-loving anarchist poet'. He was a one-time editor of the long running libertarian journal

Freedom who, towards the end of his life, was poetry editor of the communist *Morning Star* – a bit like a Spurs supporter writing the Arsenal programme notes.

Every Sunday evening, the Meeting House has a guest poet, or more often a group, coming along to read, and the event always opens with poems from the floor. The last time we were there, the advertised poet failed to turn up, so the whole evening consisted of an informal roll call of recitations, and everyone declared themselves entirely satisfied.

John Rety and Susan Johns were given the keys to 99 Torriano Avenue in 1982 by a short-life housing group which considered the building so derelict as to be beyond redemption. They managed to redeem it and established their community arts centre. Camden Council offered

a lease, and a grant which provided the means of meeting the cost. But the grant has gone and the struggle to find the £10,000 a year that the council requires is increasingly arduous.

Susan Johns provides the loving touch – the flowers in vase and jam jar, the free glass of wine – which makes the Meeting House more than simply a venue, and which gives soul to the simple surroundings. Long may it last.

6 | ROCKER'S NEWSPAPER KIOSK

Newspaper stands have never been quite so evident in London as on much of the continent. It's probably the weather. And of late, as papers' sales decline, the numbers are also against them. But the kiosk that stood for decades outside Tufnell Park tube station has a particular claim on our attention.

This newspaper stand is the subject of a memorable oil painting by the artist, Fermin Rocker. He lived close by on Anson Road for the last twenty-five or so years of his life (he died in 2004 aged 96). Both his first and last names have stories attached – he was named Fermin after a prominent Spanish anarchist and one-time mayor of Cadiz, who died a few weeks before he was born; and his father was Rudolf Rocker, the German gentile who led the sizeable Yiddish-speaking anarchist movement in London's East End in the years before the First World War.

Rocker didn't often pick local landmarks as the subject of his paintings, but this work entitled simply 'Newspaper Kiosk, Tufnell Park' is an exception. The Boston Arms looming in the background firmly locates the setting. If there was a competition for the architecturally most God awful pub in London, the Boston would have a good chance of winning. One of the remarkable aspects of this work is that it makes the pub look almost distinguished.

The pub in its current form, a traditional Irish boozer in an area awash with the gastro variety, dates from 1899 – Tufnell Park tube, with those tell-tale Edwardian-era underground station glazed tiles, from 1907, the year of Fermin Rocker's birth.

The style of the painting, and the clothes of its subjects, suggests the drab, austere mid-1950s. In fact, Rocker did not move into this area until the late 1970s, and this painting may be quite a bit later. 'From somewhere in the 1960s,' Philip Rocker comments, 'time stood still for my dad and then slowly went backwards – so fashions, cars, etc., from beyond that point are a poor indication of the date of the picture.'

Those of us who patronised the newspaper stall have fond memories of a friendly service – including one of the staff, who had clearly been collecting his pension for quite a while, who used the benediction 'there you are, young man' to customers barely clinging to middle age. The stall eventually succumbed to market pressures in the autumn of 2010, and that seemed to be the end of the line for Rocker's kiosk and the sense of community it engendered.

Not so. The following year Violet & Frederick, a better-than-average flower stall, took over the pitch. (Not to be confused with Ruby Violet, the even more up-market ice cream shop a two-minute stroll away. There are lots of Violets around here. Though the woman who runs the flower stall isn't a Violet at all, that's her mother-in-law's moniker – she has the even more interesting name of Pushkin.)

And while their stand looks brand new, it's actually the old news-paper kiosk scrubbed out, given a fresh coat of paint and with the front-age adapted for its new purpose. So, yes, Rocker's kiosk is still with us.

7 | A CELTIC SAINT

It's not what you would expect in the splendid, high church, high Victorian surroundings of St Mary Brookfield, just off Dartmouth Park Hill. But look around, and you will come across a really wonderful 600-year-old alabaster work of St Arthmael (that's the name on the plaque, but he's Armel to his admirers) – not the best known of saints, but with quite a story attached.

Armel was born in south Wales in the fifth or sixth century – his father was a Breton king. He returned to Brittany and did all the things so typical of saints of that era – killed a dragon (by drowning it in a river, as depicted bottom right), founded a few monasteries, churches and hospitals, and had a village named after him. Some historians have suggested that Armel was in fact, you've guessed it, King Arthur, who headed over to Brittany after his abdication. But even among the New Age faithful, this theory doesn't seem to have gained traction.

The cult of St Armel flourished particularly in the reign of Henry VII,

which is no doubt how a Breton saint came to be commemorated in Nottingham alabaster almost a millennium after his death. It's a charming piece, found in a loft in Llangollen in north Wales about a hundred years ago by the then vicar of St Mary's. He passed on a second piece to his brother, who was the vicar of Teddington at the time.

'It's thought that they both came from an altar piece of a medieval church in Wales which was probably destroyed at the time of the reformation or during the civil war,' says Father Guy Pope, the long-standing priest at St Mary's. 'They were subsequently hidden and probably no one realised just what they were until the twentieth century. There are traces of paint on it suggesting that it was originally highly painted which was a common practice.'

Its home is in one of the more interesting Victorian churches in north London. St Mary Brookfield (not in Brookfield at all) was established as an 1870s breakaway from St Anne's on Highgate West Hill (which is in Brookfield but now prefers to stake claim to Highgate), which wasn't all that comfortable with kids from Highgate New Town who 'looked disagreeably, smelt disagreeably, and brought fleas into the church.' St Mary's was from the start in the high church tradition, designed by the architect so closely associated with the Oxford Movement, William Butterfield, and making use of his trademark coloured bricks.

As befits its high church and anti-elitist origins, St Mary's was reputed to be the first church in the area to have free seating, with no private pews or pew rents. The roof was blown off and much of the stained glass destroyed during the Second World War, but it's been well restored and is now listed Grade II*.

Father Guy has been parish priest here for almost thirty years, and until the authors of this publication came along can only recall a solitary enquirer after the alabaster. That's close to a sin in our eyes, so let's do penance by making a pilgrimage to St Armel.

LONDON BOROU
HAR
PAR

8 | THE SMILING SUN OF HARGRAVE PARK

The squatters' movement of the 1970s has left its mark on this corner of Dartmouth Park Hill in the form of a splendid mural expressing opposition to nuclear power. Its eye-catching vantage point on the corner of Hargrave Park has made it a local landmark. The legend 'Atomic Power / No Thank You' feels a little dated, but this must be one of the earliest uses in London of the now renowned anti-nuclear smiling sun. The design originated in the Danish green movement in 1975, and this painting dates from the following year.

Local wisdom had it that the smiling sun was the handiwork of Kelvin 'the mushroom maniac', who squatted in the house he chose for his wall painting. And, as is often the way of things, the local wisdom was right.

Tracking down Kelvin took quite a while. He's been living in an old chapel in Cornwall, still determinedly opposed to nuclear power and preaching peace and love, and keen to share his account of how this smiling sun was born. So, over to Kelvin:

> How? Well, a lucky combination of circumstance I guess – a copy of [the influential 1971 book about Three Mile island] Poisoned Power: the case against nuclear power plants, a flourishing anti-nuclear movement, and me, a young headstrong hothead in those days, in love with life and convinced the world could be saved (and magic mushrooms).
>
> When? Well, I can pin that down for you too. It must have been (incredibly) 1976. Homeless and living on £5 a week, we heard of the incredible squatting movement in that area at that time – and with a massive sigh of relief we moved into that house!
>
> Why'd I graffiti me own house? Hard to say, perhaps having just got back from a nightmare demo at Aldermaston – where I'd experienced the most hideous mushroom-induced vision I'd ever had in my life – may have had something to do with it!
>
> Where? How? Having come across a few tins of old paint while on another blindingly enlightening anti-nuclear trip, I was suddenly seized with the absolute necessity to do something about it then and there – so, in the middle of the night, much to the misgivings of my long-suffering wife, and convinced I'd be getting busted for it in the morning (if not while doing it) I grabbed a ladder from a building site

opposite and dashed it off. If I'd have known that it was to last half
a lifetime I may just have taken a little more care over it.

Kelvin's legacy is a memorable piece of political street art. It's slowly fading away, but then paint doesn't have quite as long a half-life as plutonium.

9 | 'CATERING FOR BEANFEASTS'

Beanfeast – now there's a word to conjure with. 'A celebratory party with plenty of food and drink', says one online dictionary. So 'Catering for Beanfeasts', as this ghost sign on the back of a café along Highgate Road advertises, was not a task for the faint hearted.

The word derived from the custom that employers provided an annual dinner for their staff. Over time it came to refer to an employer-funded works outing, often to a beauty spot or picnic grounds. John Betjeman – who wrote about tram journeys up Highgate Road and must surely have seen this sign when it was current rather than a spectre of the past – captured in verse –

> *. . . Epping Forest glades where we*
> *Had beanfeasts with my father's firm.*
>
> (Sir John Betjeman, *Essex*)

This ghost sign overlooking the glades of Parliament Hill Fields is, then, peculiarly well placed.

Ample drink was an obligatory aspect of a good beanfeast. They were often raucous affairs. It's where the word 'beano' comes from, redolent of a good time with just a hint of excess. The nearest equivalent today is the office Christmas party – but that doesn't have a single word which wraps up every aspect of the occasion.

The sign appears on the back of 1 Highgate West Hill, which bears the more demure ghost sign 'First Class Tea Rooms Upstairs' on its flank wall. This was in the years before the First World War the site of the refreshment rooms of Capital & Counties Cafés, positioned by one of the busiest entrances to the Heath opposite Swains Lane. It's still in the

good food business – no longer tea and cakes, but the home of a popular Mediterranean-style bistro.

This appears to be about the last such visible testimony to the bean-feast. Certainly ghost sign *aficionados* know of no other. The word 'beanfeast' is now archaic – worse, it's been hijacked by purveyors of bean-based instant foods. It doesn't bear thinking about!

10 | BOROUGH CONTROL

You couldn't imagine a more insignificant looking building. It's about the size of a bus shelter, much of it painted an anonymous shade of dark brown. It has a door with no handle, no windows and contains no inscription to suggest its purpose. If any passer-by should give a moment's thought to this structure at the junction of Highgate Road and Gordon House Road, they would probably imagine it's a tool shed for the upkeep of the adjoining Highgate Enclosures, the last tiny remnant of an area of common land sometimes romantically referred to as Kentish Town's village green.

What is this? It's the entrance block to a civil defence bunker set up in the early 1950s, when the Cold War gave rise to a real fear of a nuclear conflict. This was, scarily, intended as the site of 'Camden Borough Control' if local government needed to go – quite literally – underground. The site was abandoned in the late 1960s and sealed off to keep kids out for their own safety, and has been slowly rotting away ever since.

A few years ago, the team behind the excellent Subterranea Britannica website managed to persuade Camden Council to give them access, and they have posted photos of a woefully dilapidated control centre and a plan of the installation which is reproduced here. The entrance block houses stairs which lead to an underground corridor off which there are toilets, a kitchen-cum-canteen, a plant room (the ventilation equipment and emergency generator appearing largely intact), and six other rooms.

Damp had decayed door frames and partition walls, but when inspected there were still wooden chairs and tables in what was identified as the Control Room and an electric cooker and butler sink in the kitchen. A wall-mounted ladder led to an emergency escape shaft – the

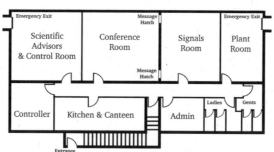

Emergency Exit		Message Hatch		Emergency Exit
Scientific Advisors & Control Room	Conference Room	Signals Room	Plant Room
		Message Hatch		
Controller	Kitchen & Canteen	Admin	Ladies	Gents
	Entrance			

Camden Borough Control Centre

exit point marked by a manhole cover in the park above. And there were two openings for passing messages between the Conference Room and the Signals Room.

The survey team reported a 'slightly oppressive atmosphere', but also noted that the bunker had no blast doors, air lock or gas protection – in other words, it would have done well to survive the sort of all-out conflict that then appeared at least a possibility.

There are some vestiges of ventilation shafts in the park – there's also a much bigger ventilation pipe, ten feet or more tall, on the other side of Highgate Road in Grove Terrace Squares, though it's not clear whether this served the bunker. What's also not clear is whether the control centre was an adaptation of a wartime air raid shelter in this same area, which included dormitories which at times housed scores of local evacuees.

The comforting aspect to this Cold War relic is that we've never had need to know that there's a nuclear bunker in NW5.

11 | THE DRAPERS' GHOST

Dartmouth Park has always been a well-heeled, well-shod sort of place, and there are still plenty of houses with a hint of Upstairs/Downstairs in their design. For the first generation of Dartmouth Park residents, having a domestic would have been a matter of course. And if you walk along York Rise, you can still see where the maids and scullery girls got kitted out.

On the side of what is now Truffles Delicatessen is one of the finest ghost signs – those eerie mementos of times and businesses past – in this part of London. The greater part of a gable wall is given over to a neatly painted advert for a drapers' and outfitters' business. It's difficult to be sure of the vintage, probably Edwardian. The sign reads:

K & M LARN / FANCY WORK / OVERALLS / BLOUSES / CORSETS / GLOVES / HOSIERY / LACES / RIBBONS / HABERDASHERY / FLANNELS / FLANNELETTES / CALICOES / UNDERCLOTHING / MAIDS' DRESSES / CAPS & APRONS

It's the mention of maids' dresses that catches the contemporary eye,

and the caps and aprons were almost certainly not for the woman of the house but for those working to her instructions. The reference to calicoes – plain-woven items made of unbleached cotton (taking their name from the port of Calicut in southern India) – is another marker of the passage of time.

And 'K & M Larn' – husband-and-wife perhaps, or maybe brothers? Wrong. A 1908 street directory lists Kate and Mildred Larn as the proprietors of this York Rise drapers' shop. The census three years later records three Larn sisters at 33 York Rise – Kate, 44, and Mildred, 35, both listed as drapers, and their younger sister Gertrude, 30, a dressmaker, and no doubt also employed in the business.

The ghost sign is protected, we're told – so it can't be covered up or defaced, though with the passage of time, it's gently fading from view.

12 | THE RIVER IN A RUSTING PIPE

'We thought for years it was a gas pipe. But it's not. It's a river.' The words of a woman walking her dog over the foot bridge across two sets of railways tracks, from the side of Acland Burghley School towards York Rise. And she's right.

The huge, ugly, rusting pipe parallel to part of the bridge carries the river Fleet, the largest and most renowned of London's lost rivers.

There are two principal tributaries of the Fleet – one from each flank of Parliament Hill. The more westerly branch rises from the Hampstead ponds on the west side of the Heath, and ran along what is now Fleet Road and through Gospel Oak.

It's the route of the other tributary, the Highgate brook, which crosses the rail lines. Its source is at the top of the Heath, more than 400 feet above sea level. The stream was repeatedly dammed in the eighteenth century to create eight large ponds, some in the grounds of Kenwood House and others now serving as the men's and women's bathing ponds. The river then made its way through Brookfield (so that's where the name came from) and towards Dartmouth Park.

The Fleet was once a much celebrated river, but became increasingly polluted by household and other waste. Concern about cholera, which prompted London's move from open to covered reservoirs, also led to the enclosure of its lesser rivers. By the 1860s, the Fleet was linked into Bazalgette's multi-level network of sewers. It had become entirely subterranean.

You can still hear it. Stand in the middle of Croftdown Road (please take care!) at the junction with Brookfield Park, and it's often clearly audible through the manhole cover. From there it flows underground, below York Rise, until it meets the two adjoining sets of railways lines. The river is piped under the more northerly lines. The second set of lines are twelve to fifteen feet lower. And for a few feet the Fleet breaks cover, within the confines of an enormous pipe, its black coating in disrepair, almost within touching distance of the foot bridge.

This is the only time the Fleet emerges from its underground lairs between the Heath and the Thames where, when in spate, it tumbles through an overspill sluice near Blackfriars Bridge.

From the railways lines, the Fleet once flowed south through Kentish Town (hence Anglers Lane) meeting up with the other tributary near Hawley Road, just north of the canal. When the river was forced underground, this remained the spot where the two streams joined – until, it

seems, the 1950s or thereabouts, when the incidence of bronchitis along the line of the Hampstead brook prompted talk of a diversion across the south of the Heath. As with so much of the detail of London's lost rivers, the exact underground route of the Fleet is not entirely clear. But it could well be the Ham and High tributaries together which force their way through the pipe across the railway lines.

The river's lasting mark is in the city's nomenclature. Not simply Fleet Road and the still more renowned Fleet Street, but also Turnmill Street in Clerkenwell . . . and quite probably our own Kentish Town, its name derived from the branch of the Fleet that flowed through it, Ken Ditch.

13 | GHANA'S REVOLUTIONARY PRESIDENT

In 1945, Kwame Nkrumah, the man who was to lead Ghana first as Prime Minister and then as President, came to live and study in London. He was then known as Francis Nkrumah, a former school teacher who had been struggling to pay his way through universities in the United States. It had been a tough time but was important in the development of his thought. Nkrumah had come into contact with a range of radical thinkers, from C. L. R. James to Marcus Garvey.

On arriving in London, Nkrumah needed somewhere to stay, and, with the help of Ako Adjei, another student from the Gold Coast (as Ghana was then known), found a room at 60 Burghley Road. English Heritage has put up a blue plaque to mark Nkrumah's temporary home. It was an ideal base, quiet yet close to the centre of London's cultural life. It was also not far from other West Africans living in Primrose Gardens in Belsize Park and close to the West African Students' Union hostel in Camden Square.

It also had another attraction: his landlady. As one biographer puts it rather coyly, she 'did not long remain exclusively in that role'. Nkrumah, although somewhat shy, was a hit with upper class English girls. He had a string of girlfriends, who were only too ready to dedicate themselves to his various causes.

Nkrumah's first political act was to support the Marxist George Padmore in his efforts to organise a Pan-African Congress in Manchester in October 1945. Nkrumah also launched the West African National

Secretariat, with the slogan 'West Africa is One Country: People of West Africa Unite!'. It was hardly a mass movement, but the one-hundred members of the Secretariat had to formally accept his leadership. Nkrumah was clearly not short of ambition. He saw himself as the President of a Union of African Socialist Republics.

Nkrumah registered at the London School of Economics for a doctorate in anthropology, but most of his time was taken up with politics. His supervisor, the philosopher A. J. Ayer recalled: 'I liked him and enjoyed talking to him but he did not seem to me to have an analytical mind.' The doctorate was never completed.

At this time the Ghanaian revolutionary was under surveillance from the British Secret Service for his membership of the British Communist Party. Yet, by a stroke of irony, it was a distinctly conservative African who possibly saved Nkrumah's life.

In 1947, he suffered a bad attack of pneumonia. A doctor was hastily summoned. He was none other than Dr Hastings Kamuzu Banda, the future President of Malawi, who at the time had a large north London practice. While Nkrumah went on to prefer flowing African robes and Marxist politics, President Banda became known for his impeccable dark three-piece suits and trade mark homburg hat and his right-wing views. 'Hippies' were banned from visiting Malawi during his rule and any man with hair judged to be too long was given a summary haircut at the border!

In the autumn of that year, Nkrumah left for Ghana to re-engage with politics back home. Within months the British had fired on a march by ex-servicemen and arrested Nkrumah, assuming he was behind the agitation. Although he was not, it did his reputation no end of good, and the charismatic Nkrumah rapidly rose to lead the movement for independence from Britain. Five years after leaving Burghley Road, he was his country's Prime Minister, and within a decade he had led Ghana to independence.

14 | THE GREAT WAR IN COLLEGE LANE

College Lane, which runs parallel to Highgate Road, is the most intriguing and least conventional street in NW5. The houses – built piecemeal, as you can tell from the range of styles and designs – don't open on to a road, but a path. And only the west side of the path has been developed.

A map of the 1860s shows the first few houses on what was then a cart track overlooking green fields. The houses were smaller than many in the area, and became home to rail workers in particular. Longer established residents remember than in the 1970s there were still three rail workers and their families living on College Lane. And through the second half of the last century, the rail workers' social club here – the site long awaiting redevelopment – reinforced the association.

You can walk along College Lane many times without spotting the small war memorial, a plaque just above head height on the wall of numbers 13 and 14. It's reputed to be the only First World War memorial in London mounted on a house. St Pancras Borough Council, it appears, wanted to honour the war dead by dedicating a hospital ward. College Lane wanted a more local and enduring remembrance of their family, friends and neighbours.

The shield-shaped plaque is so weathered, and has been painted over so many times down the decades, it's no longer completely legible. But the ten names can still be read. And the war historian Carl Crane, the secretary of the Old Comrades' Association of the St Pancras-raised 19th London Regiment in which the men served, has pieced together their stories.

All died in the fighting in Flanders or northern France:

Private John Albert Powell Sayers, killed in action in September 1915
Private Fred Britcher, killed in action in September 1916
Private Charles James Manning, died from his wounds
Private William James Cecil Stratton, killed in action in July 1916 aged
*   25*
Private Douglas Walter Barrett, killed in action in March 1917 aged 26
Private Harry Janes, died from his wounds in December 1917
Rifleman Percy Robert Leahey, died of his wounds in August 1917
Private Charles Henry Biggs, killed in action aged 33
Private William Henry Turner, died from his wounds in July 1917

Lieutenant-Sergeant Alfred Herbert Stanton, died from his wounds in October 1918

Scouring the 1911 census records reveals just how local these war dead were. Alfred Stanton, a metalworker operating a capstan lathe, was then lodging at 1 College Grove, one of eleven people in the household. Percy Leahey was a name shared by a father and son at 16 College Lane, one a printer and the other an errand boy, part of a family of ten.

And the memorial wasn't placed on numbers 13 and 14 simply because these were among the most imposing houses on the Lane. The Strattons were one of two households living at no. 14, according to the 1911 census. The head of household is listed as a glass fitter in the cabinet trade, and it's probably his son or close relative who is remembered in the memorial.

The current residents of College Lane continue to honour the memory of those who fell a century ago by placing a poppy on the plaque every November.

15 | ST MARTIN'S – STILL CRAZY AFTER ALL THESE YEARS

St Martin's wears Nikolaus Pevsner's label as a badge of honour. After all, being called crazy by Britain's leading architectural historian does make you stand apart from the crowd. St Martin's, Gospel Oak, does, indeed, stand out – you can spot it from the Heath with its narrow, awkward, unfinished looking tower which always sports the St George's flag (an entirely innocent tradition insists the vicar, Chris Brice).

Pevsner's description of St Martin's as 'the craziest of London's Victorian churches' is not simply on the front page of the church's illustrated history – it's cited in the very first line. St Martin's also has the rare accolade for a suburban parish church of a Grade 1 listing. It's the only church on our patch to feature in Simon Jenkins's *England's Thousand Best Churches*. And it wins a place in Elizabeth and Wayland Young's *London Churches* – though they go on to add (and again this is quoted in the church's own guide which clearly has embraced the 'warts and all' approach):

To include this church is not an expression of the authors' liking or
approval: rather an expression of faith in the oddness of the human,
and therefore of the divine, imagination. Thus must Adam have felt on
first seeing the duck-billed platypus.

Holy cow!

If you don't know St Martin's, that's forgivable. While most parish churches were built on a busy junction, this one is on a back street – and after the post-war rebuilding of Gospel Oak (the windswept, desolate Lismore Circus is close by), a back street to nowhere in particular, though how wonderfully appropriate to have a church on Vicars Road.

St Martin's was built in the 1860s through the munificence of an evangelical glove magnate from the Midlands. He employed as architect

Edward Buckton Lamb, whose approach is generously described by the church history as 'idiosyncratic' and by others in his profession as 'rogue'.

The interior is what excites ecclesiastical historians – a magnificent wooden roof, alabaster in profusion, mosaic panels, and happily some of the Morris & Co stained glass survived wartime bombing.

But it's the thin, asymmetrical tower that makes its mark on most visitors. What they may not realise is that the original design was even more outlandish – and is set to return to the north London skyline.

The top of the tower has for years been unadorned, but originally there were corner pinnacles, and a remarkable turret straight out of the Brothers Grimm. These were brought down by wartime damage, or were so unsafe they were removed in subsequent years. Chris Brice has been trying to track down as many images, drawings and plans as he can of the initial design . . . because St Martin's is in for Heritage Lottery money to restore the tower to its fairyland Gothic glory.

Of late, the tower has been swathed in scaffolding, and on the church door a notice announces that the work is for the 'reinstatement of four pinnacles and corner tower to original designs'. Crazier and crazier!

16 | AT HOME WITH KARL MARX

In October 1856, Karl Marx and his wife Jenny were able to leave the squalor of Soho and move up to newly fashionable Kentish Town. They had arrived in London in May 1849, taking up residence in Dean Street. As German revolutionaries they had been on the move for years, having left Brussels, Paris and Cologne behind them. London was a sanctuary and Karl Marx was to live and work here for the rest of his life.

Jenny, the daughter of a Prussian Baron, described her Soho home as consisting of 'evil, frightful rooms'. By contrast, she loved the new house at 9 Grafton Terrace and wrote of it as 'a magic castle . . . at the foot of romantic Hampstead Heath, not far from lovely Primrose Hill'. The street has been renumbered, and the Marx family home has been variously suggested to be the current numbers 36, 38 or 48 – though the consensus is that 46 Grafton Terrace (and how appropriate that it now has a vivid red front door) is Jenny's little bit of north London magic,

46

and its curving steps, railings, and balustrades bear just the faintest touch of a fairy tale fortress.

The move had been made possible by two inheritances by Jenny of £270. The house was rented for £36 a year and Karl made sure he paid the rates (£4.20) on time. But the family was soon back in debt and a year later Karl Marx was complaining that he was 'wallowing in the very quintessence of filth'. Karl tried to bring in some income, but his application to become a clerk on the Great Western Railway was turned down; his handwriting was illegible.

In the winter of 1863, Karl inherited a substantial sum from his mother and an old friend and moved again, this time to 1 Modena Villas, today re-named Maitland Park Road. It was a really substantial property, with a rent of £65. Karl could enjoy the benefits of a book-lined study 'stacked up to the ceiling with newspapers and manuscripts'. There the family could live in some style, with two dogs, three cats and two birds. The girls, Jenny, Laura and Eleanor, who were educated at South Hampstead Ladies' College, held a ball for their friends.

The Marx family settled down to a pleasant routine in their new surroundings. They took weekend picnics onto the Heath, reading the Sunday papers or snoozing after lunch. They walked to Sadler's Wells to see Shakespeare's plays performed. Karl was particularly fond of patronising local pubs, including Jack Straw's Castle.

In 1870 Karl's great friend, patron and collaborator, Frederich Engels finally sold his factory in Manchester (a 'shitty business' as he described it) and moved to London. He bought a house just down the road from the Marx household at 122 Regent's Park Road, Primrose Hill. It cost the not inconsiderable sum of £12,500. Jenny Marx, who found it for the Engels family, wrote: 'I have now found a house, which charms all of us because of its wonderful open situation. It is next to Primrose Hill, so all the front rooms have the finest and openest view and air. And round about, in the side streets, there are shops of all sorts, so your wife will be able to buy everything herself.'

The final move for the Marx family came in 1875. By this time his chief work *Capital* had been published in German and Russian and was selling well. They moved to 41 Maitland Park Road. While this house, like Modena Villas, has vanished, the family's residence is commemorated by a brown commemorative plaque, courtesy of Camden Council. Set high on the side of a block of Council flats, it states simply: 'Karl

Marx, 1818–1883. Philosopher. Lived and died in a House on this Site, 1875–1883.'

Karl Marx was buried in Highgate cemetery in the same grave as his wife, Jenny, who had died fifteen months earlier. In 1954 they were reinterred in a more prominent position, and two years later the bronze bust which currently marks the site was unveiled, sculpted by Laurence Bradshaw and commissioned by the Communist Party of Great Britain. It rests on a huge Cornish granite plinth bearing one of Marx's more memorable aphorisms: 'Philosophers have only interpreted the world in various ways – The point however is to change it.'

17 | THE SECRET HORSE TUNNELS OF CAMDEN LOCK

How many of the ten-million tourists who flock to Camden Lock every year, picking through the clothes or sampling a pizza, realise they stand on one of the rarest examples of industrial archaeology? Beneath their feet lies a complex system of horse tunnels.

At the height of its operation, the Lock employed more than 400 horses. Horses and carts were used extensively on the site, moving goods to and from the railways that ran into the Camden Goods Depot. The depot was developed from 1839 as the London terminus of the London and Birmingham Railway, the capital's first inter-city main line railway. Goods were then transported onwards to London's docks via the railways and the Regent's Canal. The twenty-five acre site was, in its day, a truly integrated transport hub and the largest civil engineering project attempted in the country.

The future of the site was assured by Walter Gilbey who was persuaded by the railways to move his company onto it. He had founded W & A Gilbey Ltd in 1857 to import the wine of South Africa to serve a growing Victorian market. The firm thrived, becoming the largest drinks firm in the world. Every day a train, the 'Gilbey's Special', left for the docks to supply distant markets around the world with the gin for which the firm had become famous.

Life for the horses working in and around Camden Lock was difficult and dangerous and they were frequently hit by trains. To increase their

safety and to allow ease of movement, two horse tunnels were constructed around 1855. Each had several spurs, leading to warehouses or the canal.

The western tunnel led from the London and North Western Railway stables next to the canal at Fitzroy Bridge in Primrose Hill – an area bounded by Gloucester Avenue and Princess Road. Today the stables have been replaced by modern flats, next to the Engineer pub. This is the only part of the tunnel system which was accessible to the public until quite recently. It was partly incorporated into the Italian restaurant on Gloucester Avenue, Sardo Canale. Sadly, the restaurant has now closed. The tunnel ran under the railway, surfacing just opposite what was Pickford's shed.

The eastern tunnel ran from Oval Road, just west of the Interchange basin, under the railway, surfacing close to the New Stables (built in 1881–3) and giving easy access to the nearby Horse Hospital (constructed in 1889) adjacent to Hampstead Road.

The tunnels are round-arched 10 ft (3.0 m) wide by 9 ft (2.7 m) high and large sections of them still exist, even if they are not accessible to the public. But if you go behind the Interchange warehouse you can still see a few of the ventilation grilles set into the cobbles. The cast iron grilles were placed about 10 ft or 3.0 m apart in the roof, and were originally the only source of light.

The companies that used the horses were proud of their animals and entered them into local horse shows. Gilbey's in particular was famous for its horses, breeding prize-winning Shires and winning many prizes. Walter Gilbey also campaigned to improve the treatment of the animals, founding the London Cart Horse Parade in 1885. Its successor, the London Harness Horse Parade, exists to this day, competing in shows around England.

A local website, Camdenworld blog, records this touching anecdote:

Mr L. King, now an elderly man, wrote to me saying:
'As young lads we used to go up to the railway stables and the carters would give us rubbing brushes. After a day's work those horses would be tethered, watered and fed and we made their coats shine.
'Or we went to the Barracks in Albany Road. We got in there too. The sentries let us in and sometimes we used to be lucky when the horses

came back. They used to do ceremonial guards at Buckingham Palace and all that sort of place. The soldiers came back and dismounted and again they let us help to clean the horses and feed them and give them their nosebags.

'We did work hard. They were really well treated, those horses. It was VIP treatment for them.'

18 | THE ARTIST COLONY IN PRIMROSE HILL

Leave the tempting bistros and boutiques of Regent's Park Road behind, stroll past the neatly pollarded plane trees that line Berkley Road down to Chalcot Square. Crossing the square and avoiding the urge to enjoy a beer in The Princess of Wales, turn right into Fitzroy Road. Soon you find number 23 on the left. Here Ireland's greatest poet, W. B. Yeats, lived as a child (1867 to 1873), a fact marked by a blue plaque. The house was also later home to Sylvia Plath, who moved there from Chalcot Square. A little further up the road and a small opening appears between the houses – surmounted by a slightly dilapidated but rather fine sign: 'Primrose Hill Studios' and then just below, 'Private Road, No Parking'.

Passing under the pedimented sign you enter another world. Here are a group of twelve cottage-style houses around a quiet garden courtyard. They were constructed between 1870 and 1872 by Alfred Healey, a local builder. It was the last major development in the area. According to Caroline Ramsden, a resident from 1935, Healey himself lived at 49 Fitzroy Road. Perhaps the young Yeats played among the sand and bricks as the cottages went up.

The studios were purpose-built for artists, with generous windows and high skylights to let in as much light as possible. There was a lodge near the entrance, home to servants and a keeper who supervised the buildings and provided meals. Ramsden recalls in her memoir, *A View from Primrose Hill*, that: 'Double gates at the top of the entry were locked at night by the caretaker and residents on an evening out, who forgot to take their keys, had to ring the lodge bell in Kingstown Street, and be admitted through the side gate.'

A total of thirty-nine artists worked at Primrose Hill Studios from 1878 to 1899. Some also lived there with their families and the community

was said to be inspired by a camaraderie reflecting the egalitarian art-worker ideal promoted by Ruskin and Morris. Many went on to become members of the St John's Wood Arts Club, inaugurated in 1895.

English Heritage has helpfully provided details of some of the first residents. They are an impressive group:

The painter John Dawson Watson (1832–1892, lived at no. 1) came from Sedbergh, Yorkshire and illustrated Daniel Defoe's *Robinson Crusoe* and the *Arabian Nights*.

The Prussian artist, Joseph Wolf (1820–1899, no. 2), was famous for his vivid wildlife drawings. He received many commissions, including from the Zoological Society of London in nearby Regent's Park.

John William Waterhouse RA (1849–1917, first lived at no. 3 then no. 6) was a member of the Pre-Raphaelite school of painters. Among his studies was 'La Belle Dame Sans Merci', which he worked on in 1893. The painting was exhibited at the Royal Academy of Arts, receiving considerable praise.

John Charles Dollman (1851–1934, no. 5) from Hove, produced many paintings that were well-known in their time, including some based on Rudyard Kipling's stories, among them 'Mowgli made leader of the Bandar-log'.

Peregrine M. Feeney (1837–1913, no. 7) was Birmingham born, a fine landscape painter and a close friend of John William Waterhouse.

Charles Whymper, (1853–1941, no. 8) illustrated books on travel, sport and natural history.

Later tenants were just as interesting and talented. The famous illustrator Arthur Rackham lived at no. 3 in 1905–6 and then at no. 6, when some of the books of the Brother Grimm's fairy tales, for which he is best known, were published.

Lord Methuen, (1886–1974, no. 6) landscape and figure painter, and trustee of the Tate was another. His paintings included an evocative work 'London by Moonlight, Primrose Hill', a view of the old piano factory just opposite the Studios. A later resident of the same property was the artist Patrick Caulfield (1936–2005), known for his use of bold colours and photorealism.

Caroline Ramsden (no. 8) was a writer and sculptor, who recalled the bombing of the studios in September 1940. 'The studio's nearest bomb descended – a quite junior affair. It knocked down a wall and made a small crater in Kingstown Street, mussed up the lodge, which was fortunately empty at the time, and turned our overhead telephone wires into something resembling a piece of knitting which has been played with by a kitten. No one was hurt in the process.' The photograph of the bombing shows a good deal of damage, but Caroline was of a tougher generation than ours, which did not make a fuss.

John Hoyland, (no 10) from Sheffield (1934–2011) was one of Britain's leading abstract expressionist painters.

The courtyard was not just home to artists. Sir Henry Wood, (1869–1944, no. 5) musician, conductor and creator of the Proms, also lived here. Martita Hunt (1899–1969, no. 7), born in Buenos Aires to British parents, was a noted actress, performing on the stage and in films. She is perhaps best known for her portrayal of Miss Havisham in the 1946 production of *Great Expectations*.

Perhaps the most intriguing of all the Studios' residents was a Russian Prince, Elim Pavlovich Demidov-San Donato, (1874–1941). The inheritor of a vast fortune founded on iron smelting, and reputedly the richest man in Europe, Prince Demidoff (as he is sometimes known) was a naturalist, author and big game hunter. He served as a diplomat with the Russian embassy in London from 1894. He wrote about his exploits as a hunter, with books such as *After Wild Sheep in the Altai and Mongolia*, published in 1900, followed by *A Shooting Trip to Kamchatka* in 1904.

Prince Demidoff was assigned to the Russian embassy in Madrid in 1902 and then to Copenhagen the following year. From 1905 he served as first secretary in Vienna and then in Paris and finally as ambassador in Athens (1912–17). Unsurprisingly, he did not return to Russia following the 1917 revolution.

19 | READY MONEY DRINKING FOUNTAIN

'Ready Money Drinking Fountain' it says on the map as you enter Regent's Park . . . which must confuse those who, on finding this exceptionally ornate mid-Victorian red granite and marble fountain in the park's Broad Walk, can see no ready money to hand or indeed mentioned.

The fountain has been spruced up, with the help of lottery money (perhaps that's the ready money?), and still spouts water – courtesy of infra-red technology. The inscription, though, is rooted in another era. The fountain was inaugurated in 1869 by H.R.H. Princess Mary, Duchess of Teck – a Hanover-born cousin of Queen Victoria who, it's said, had some difficulty finding a spouse, eventually settling for a penniless princeling from Wurttemberg. Their daughter, another Mary, married George V.

The benefactor has an even better back story. This fountain was the gift of Sir Cowasjee Jehangir, 'a wealthy Parsee gentleman of Bombay as a token of gratitude to the people of England for the protection enjoyed by him and his Parsee fellow countrymen under the British rule in India'. This was little more than a decade after the 1857 Indian Rebellion (or Mutiny), a turning point in Britain's Imperial history.

Parsees – followers of the Zoroastrian faith originally from Persia, hence the name – were a small but hugely influential community in nineteenth century Bombay (now Mumbai). The first three Indian members of the House of Commons were all Parsees – elected respectively in the Liberal, Conservative and Communist interest. They were prominent in finance and commerce, and indeed Sir Cowasjee Jehangir's forbears had made a fortune particularly out of the lucrative opium trade to China, so much so that they embraced the term 'Readymoney' not simply as a nickname but as their surname. And their home was Readymoney House in Bombay's elite Malabar Hill district.

Some time in the twentieth century, the family thought better of the 'Readymoney' sobriquet and dropped it from the family name. And perhaps it was strait-laced prudery which kept the slightly vulgar 'Readymoney' off the fountain's plaque. If so, it didn't work. The fountain, one of the grandest in London, is now universally known after its benefactor's missing surname. And on the south side, weathered but still clear to see, is a likeness of Sir Cowasjee, with his splendid moustache and bald dome peering out towards the city.

20 | MATILDA THE ABSURD

Virginia Woolf described this as 'an absurd statue' – at least, it's likely this is the one she had in mind as she recounts a walk in and around Regent's Park in *Mrs Dalloway*. And it's difficult to disagree.

This corner of NW1, indeed, is overburdened with the absurd. Just a few yards away is the bridge over nowhere, which also features among our curiosities. And here's this rural idyll on the north side of Gloucester Gate on top of a great big rockery – so big that the girl's feet are on about the same level as the heads of passers-by . . . a bronze statue perhaps of a milkmaid, perhaps a girl gathering water at a spring, who is gazing forlornly on the sylvan swathes of the park.

The close-to-life-size bronze has a certain rustic charm – though why a simple drinking fountain should be graced by such a fancy piece of work, heaven alone knows. The Cornish rocks on which the statue rests are not so much a cairn, as a full-blown grotto, almost a cave. In the hollow is what would once have been the drinking fountain, hewn from a large stone, though by the look of it no water has poured forth for a very long time. Perhaps the girl is not peering wistfully, but scouring anxiously for somewhere else to fill-up her bucket.

The maid is the handiwork of Joseph Durham, a hotshot sculptor of the time and regular exhibitor at the Royal Academy. He designed the statue of Prince Albert, Queen Victoria's consort, now outside the Royal Albert Hall. Durham's speciality was boys engaged in athletic exercises, but he also made a series of statues of girls in this same style, shading their eyes, pail at their feet, as they look gracefully into the distance. There's a very similar Durham bronze in Blackburn Town Hall. This must have been one of his last works. He died in 1877, the year before this fountain was installed.

According to the plaque, the edifice was presented to the Metropolitan Drinking Fountain Association (this organisation survives though without the 'Metropolitan' in its title and sponsors the online www.findafountain.org) in August 1878 by Matilda, wife of Richard Kent who was then St Pancras's junior churchwarden. So it has inevitably become known as the Matilda Fountain, though for the avoidance of doubt, it's not Matilda up there. That would just be too absurd!

21 | A BRIDGE OVER NOTHING

Families strolling to the Zoo from Camden tube, passing the restaurants and estate agents on Parkway, will probably have their hands full keeping track of their children. As they make their way over Prince Albert Road and approach Regent's Park, how many will notice the bridge they are crossing? If they glance over the ornate cast iron parapet they might wonder briefly why it was built, since it crosses nothing but grass and young trees. But the Zoo beckons and the children will be tugging at their hands; there is little time to stop and stare.

Gloucester Gate Bridge, as the red and purple brick structure is known, is beautifully detailed, with significant works of art, but why is it there?

It once really served a purpose, crossing a spur of the Regent's Canal that ran south into Cumberland Basin. This section of the canal was built in 1813–16, running to the east of Regent's Park and Albany Street and ending at Cumberland Market.

Barges carried hay and straw for sale in the market. This was how the horses at the nearby Albany Street army barracks were kept in comfort. Each barge carried up to thirty tonnes. They brought stone and lime for building works, as well as coal and timber for the coach building and furniture trades.

Cumberland Basin was once nearly as large as Battlebridge Basin near Kings Cross. The flats overlooking the basin were built in the 1920s and '30s as 'homes fit for heroes' who returned after the horrors of the First World War.

It was in the Second World War that Cumberland Basin fell into decline. During 1942–3 the canal was used to draw water to fight the fires caused by German bombing. As houses in the area were destroyed during the Blitz, the rubble was thrown into the canal, until the basin was filled. Top soil was brought from Windsor Castle and today it is used for allotments.

The rest of the spur leading from the Regent's Canal was also filled in. All that is left is the stump where the Feng Shang Princess floating Chinese restaurant is moored.

So it is that Gloucester Gate Bridge crosses nothing more than a gentle dip in the ground. Despite this the bridge boasts a fine sculpture, known as 'Matilda' (see the previous entry) and two matching bronze

59

panels depicting the martyrdom of Saint Pancras. Originally crafted by the artist C. E. Fucigna, and remodelled by the sculptor Stuart Smith, the panels portray the martyrdom of St Pancras, a Roman who was fed to the lions for his faith. Impressed by the young man's holiness, the beasts refused to attack, until he gave them permission to kill him.

This depiction is something of a mistake. The real Saint Pancras was a martyr killed during the persecution of Christians by the Emperor Diocletian, around 303 AD. He is thought to have been decapitated, not fed to the lions!

The bridge itself was constructed by the firm Kirk and Randall. It was commissioned by William Booth Scott, engineer for the Vestry of St Pancras, as the borough was then known, and opened in August 1877.

22 | THE ANTIDOTE TO BLUE PLAQUES

Question: 'Why is there a blue plaque to Willie Rushton in Mornington Crescent tube station?'

Answer: 'I'm sorry I haven't a clue.'

That might not be up to Barry Cryer's standard of wit and repartee ('oh yes it is!', I hear the other panellists exclaim), but if it raises a ghost of a smile, then you know what we're on about.

As you go past the ticket barriers at Mornington Crescent, there's a small plaque put up by Comic Heritage: 'Willie Rushton, 1937–1996, Satirist'. Rushton, with a bunch of his chums from Shrewsbury School, founded *Private Eye* in 1961, and the following year again pushed the boundaries as part of the topical TV satirical show 'That was the week that was'.

In the 1970s, radio beckoned. 'I'm Sorry I Haven't a Clue', proud to declare itself 'the antidote to panel games', took to the Radio 4 airwaves in 1972, and two years later Willie Rushton became a regular on this gently anarchic comedy programme. He remained one of its linchpins until his death in 1996.

As Radio 4 fans will know, 'Mornington Crescent' has been a highlight of 'I'm Sorry I Haven't a Clue' for more years than there are stations on the Bank branch. Panellists take turns to name London locations, usually tube stations, until one of them winningly declares: 'Mornington Crescent'. This might suggest that logic and London lore play a part in the contest. That's quite wrong. Several rule books have been published, participants often refer to the game's regulations and to their strategies much as if this is grandmaster chess. But there is no rhyme or reason to 'Mornington Crescent', at least none that can be codified, which is of course its chief delight.

According to the late Humphrey Lyttelton, for many years the show's chairman, 'Mornington Crescent' was devised with the purpose of outsmarting a particularly unpopular producer. 'Quick,' said one panellist as this producer approached. 'Let's invent a game with rules he'll never

understand.' But that's probably about as reliable as the Northern Line on Christmas Day.

What may have a touch more truth to it is that this Radio 4 'antidote' saved the real Mornington Crescent station. It was closed for much of the 1990s for renovation, and there were suggestions that it was quietly being mothballed – but a campaign, spurred on by its Radio 4 fame, ensured that Mornington Crescent came back to life. And in April 1998, six years after its temporary closure, the 'I'm Sorry I Haven't a Clue' team turned up for the reopening ceremony.

'It's not generally known,' Humphrey Lyttelton declared, 'but the area of the station is actually named after the game and not the other way around. The game goes back to Roman times' . . . to which Tim Brooke-Taylor responded: 'The lifts go back to Roman times, but only if you press the bottom button.'

In March 2002, veteran panellists and 'Mornington Crescent' contestants, including Barry Cryer, Graeme Garden and Tim Brooke-Taylor, returned to the station to unveil this tribute to their former colleague.

So as they say on 'I'm Sorry I Haven't a Clue': 'Mornington Crescent!' – cue laughter and applause.

23 | THE STRANGEST OF POETS

In September 1872, two Frenchmen arrived in London. Although the city has seen some extraordinary visitors, few can match Paul Verlaine and Arthur Rimbaud. Today they are recognised as some of their country's most illustrious and important poets, but their lifestyles were – well – remarkable.

Arthur Rimbaud was an angelic looking, rebellious anarchist. His drinking and unruly behaviour shocked many people, to his evident delight. Paul Verlaine, ten years his senior, was smitten by the young man when he turned up on his doorstep in 1871. Verlaine, already a drinker, was soon led astray by his youthful friend. They descended into a life of writing and arguments, fuelled by absinthe and hashish.

The two became lovers; Verlaine left his wife and travelled to London. They stayed a night or two in Soho before finding rooms in Howland Street in Fitzrovia, where they mixed with other French refugees.

Verlaine helped with a left-wing paper, *L'Avenir,* and they attended meetings in Soho at which another émigré, Karl Marx, frequently spoke.

Rimbaud was 'delighted and astonished' by London. Verlaine was overwhelmed by what he described as the 'incessant railways on splendid cast-iron bridges' and the 'brutal, loud-mouthed people in the streets', but inspired by the 'interminable docks'.

When they were not writing, they followed their twin passions: walking and the city's nightlife. They explored the city tirelessly on foot, visiting Crystal Palace, Hyde Park, Kew. At Limehouse in the East End, they tried opium after reading Thomas De Quincey. They were also ardent theatregoers seeing Shakespeare, Sheridan and enjoying the music of Offenbach.

Rimbaud wrote:

I am a temporary and not discontented citizen
Of a metropolis considered modern because all known taste has
   been eluded
In furnishings or the outsides of the houses,
As well as in the plan of the city.

Here you will find no trace of a single monument to superstition.
Morals and language have been reduced
   To their simplest expression, that is all!

He celebrated his eighteenth birthday in London, spending his days exploring poetry in the Reading Room of the British Museum. He possibly sat close to Marx, who was also using the great library at the time.

The poets moved between Belgium and London over the next three years. In May 1873 they are back in London again, this time living in Camden, at 8 Royal College Street (where a plaque records their stay). Quite what their landlady, a Mrs Smith, made of her tenants is not recorded.

Verlaine describes Camden as 'a gay district which reminds one of Brussels'. He enjoyed the close proximity of Kentish Town and Hampstead Heath. 'I go there often when I don't go to the Reading Room of the British Museum,' he wrote. He and Rimbaud went to see the Shah of Persia make a state ride through London.

Rimbaud worked on *A Season in Hell,* today hailed as a modernist masterpiece, while Verlaine began writing the poems 'Spleen,' 'Green' and 'Street'. But their relationship was nothing if not tempestuous. The lovers frequently disagreed and these altercations were sometimes violent and often physical. 'I know these passions and disasters too well,' Rimbaud wrote in 1873, 'the rages, the debauches, the madness'.

The final straw came when Verlaine arrived back home one evening after fetching the ingredients for the couple's evening meal at Camden Market. Verlaine was carrying herring. Rimbaud sniggered at Verlaine and told him that he looked a fool. After months of insults, Verlaine finally had enough, turned and left. He hailed a cab to St. Katharine's Docks where he took the next ferry to Calais. Rimbaud attempted to find Verlaine, but was too late.

Verlaine, overcome with grief, wrote to Rimbaud threatening suicide. After pawning his lover's clothes, Rimbaud followed him and, in a Brussels hotel, they had their final row. With the gun with which he'd planned to kill himself, Verlaine shot Rimbaud in the wrist. He was jailed for two years, during which time he converted to Catholicism. Verlaine visited Britain later in his life, but his final years were marked by drug addiction, alcoholism and poverty and he died in Paris in 1896.

Yet he was to have one final major link with Britain: on 1 June 1944 the opening lines of his 1866 poem Autumn Song were broadcast on the BBC.

The long sobs
of autumn's
violins
wound my heart
with a monotonous
languor.

These lines were for the French Resistance, informing them that the D-Day landings were imminent and the liberation of Europe was about to begin.

After the shooting, Rimbaud left Europe and travelled to the Horn of Africa, living in the remote Ethiopian city of Harar, trading coffee and guns. He returned to France in 1891, dying of cancer and is buried in his native town of Charleville-Mézières.

Today the two poets are celebrated as among France's most important poets, influencing the Symbolists, Dadaists, and Surrealists.

24 | TWO SOUTH AFRICAN REVOLUTIONARIES

In 1965, a South African couple were lucky enough to have their parents buy them a modest property in Camden, at 13 Lyme Street. Although the street was just off busy Camden Road, it was actually a quiet refuge for the family. But Joe Slovo and Ruth First were no ordinary émigrés: members of the South African Communist Party, they were at the heart of the fight against apartheid.

Joe had been a lawyer, defending ANC leaders by day, while plotting the overthrow of the regime by night. Ruth was a journalist. Both had seen the inside of prison, with Ruth's jailer mockingly remarking 'bye, bye blue sky' as she was led away in 1963. She served 117 days in detention without trial, only to be freed after the intervention of Helen Suzman, then the sole liberal Member of Parliament.

The following year, forbidden from practising in court, Joe slipped across the Botswana border. Ruth followed him to London, leaving the country of her birth on an exit visa. It was to be three decades before Joe was to see South Africa again; Ruth never did.

They settled into their life in Camden, with Joe working full time for the ANC and the communists. He divided his time between three offices close to Tottenham Court Road. 39 Goodge Street was the shabby office of the exiled Communist Party and the ANC office was just around the corner at 49–51 Rathbone Street. The Anti-Apartheid Movement was nearby at 89 Charlotte Street. Joe would lunch with Ronnie Kasrils – a fellow party member – at a Greek restaurant, Georges. The men would bet on the outcome of football matches. Ronnie was an Arsenal supporter, Joe backed Chelsea. 'It was so funny because I never, ever had to buy him lunch,' Kasrils recalls.

While Joe was attempting to resuscitate the ANC's moribund armed struggle, travelling constantly to the Soviet Union and the party's bases in Africa, Ruth took up a successful academic career. She became an editor of the *Review of African Political Economy*, advised the United Nations and published a string of books. She also was an effective speaker at anti-apartheid rallies in Trafalgar Square.

Both were so engaged in their careers there was little time for their three daughters: Shawn, Gillian (who based her novel, *Ties of Blood*, on her family history) and Robyn. Despite this, life in Camden was not

without its fun. Ruth was an excellent cook and the couple were known for the parties they threw.

There were also fierce, bitter rows; sometimes over money, sometimes over Joe's contribution to the household chores, which Ruth suggested amounted to making the salad dressing. The two gradually drifted apart. Joe was an unreconstructed Stalinist, who believed that ANC members should be put through the rigours of East Germany's Lenin School to 'refashion their minds', as Ronnie Kasrils later recalled. Ruth, who trained with Ralph Miliband at the London School of Economics, was drawn to the Marxism of the New Left. She supported a variety of causes that the ANC disapproved of, including Eritrean independence.

By 1977 the couple had gone their separate ways, but both found their way to Africa. Joe ended up at the ANC's headquarters in Lusaka, while Ruth went to Mozambique, where she taught at the university. Her career was brought to a tragic end in August 1982, when a letter bomb sent by the apartheid regime killed her in Maputo. Joe was to return to South Africa in 1990, by then Communist Party general secretary. Finally acknowledging the excesses of Stalinism, he played a major role in shaping the newly democratic country until his death from cancer in 1995.

25 | THE ELEPHANT HOUSE

No, not the one in the Zoo – the other, better, Elephant House on our patch. If you are on the top deck of the C2 heading north from Camden tube station, then look left just after you cross Hawley Crescent and you will come eye-to-eye with an elephant. An exquisite elephant head in profile, replete with tusk and trunk, crafted in sandstone – the stand-out feature of a distinctly smart building.

The head is above the door on Kentish Town Road, on the side aspect of the building. The bigger frontage is on Hawley Crescent – at the top there's a date stone, '1900' it reads, and between the numerals the mischievous, unmistakable curve of an elephant's trunk, and there was once an elephant's head in profile on this aspect too.

Camden Brewery developed the site as a bottle store with an adjoining coopers' building (the guys that made the wooden beer barrels). William Bradford, the architect, was renowned for giving breweries, industrial premises after all, a bit of style – here using striking red brick and terracotta to lift this building well above the standard of your common-or-garden bottling plant. It's also one of the few industrial buildings to survive alongside the Regent's Canal, which was of course built as a transport network. The brewery itself was on the same site, but older – the business dated back to 1859 – and next-to-nothing of it survives.

And the elephant? Well, that was the trademark of Camden Brewery and one of their most popular brews was Elephant's Head Pale Ale.

The brewery closed in the 1920s, and the building, listed a few years back, is now part of the European headquarters of Viacom, the multinational that brings us MTV among other things. The connection with the licensed trade continues, not so much with 'The Dev' immediately opposite, that well known Goth haunt The Devonshire Arms, but with the pub at the Camden High Street end of the Crescent, the – you've got it – Elephant's Head.

In recent years, of course, Camden Town Brewery has been reborn and is famed above all for its Hell's Lager. It's based not all that far away, close to West Kentish Town station. And in a nice tribute to its predecessor, for the 2012 Olympics the new brewery turned to a recipe in the older one's archives for a beer that took the name '1908', the year London first hosted the games.

26 | WHEN BATHS WERE BATHS

In the 1980s, it was still possible to find homes in Kentish Town that had no baths or showers. Local people either used 'flannel baths' – soaping themselves down with a flannel – or they went down the road to a much loved institution: the Kentish Town Baths. Situated on Prince of Wales Road, it provided clean baths to anyone who needed them. You paid for the privilege and went upstairs, where a tub of hot water would be run and then the hot tap removed! It was a certain means of ensuring that you got on with the business of cleaning yourself. There was little chance that you would loll about, luxuriating in fast-cooling water.

A far larger number of residences did not have a washing machine, so the baths provided these too. Entering from Grafton Road you faced a series of industrial size washing machines plus dryers and giant

rollers, for ironing your sheets. It was a convivial place, where local people (mainly women) met and talked as they did their washing.

Thanks to the research of the former Labour councillor, Gerry Harrison, for the *Camden History Review*, we know a great deal more about the baths and how they came about. The Kentish Town Baths were not the first in Camden (then known as St Pancras). That honour goes to baths on North Gower Street, which opened in 1847 but were considered inadequate and closed just thirteen years later.

In 1894, the site of Prince of Wales Baths was purchased for £18,000. A competition for the design was held and won by Thomas W. Aldwinckle, described as 'an experienced London architect of the

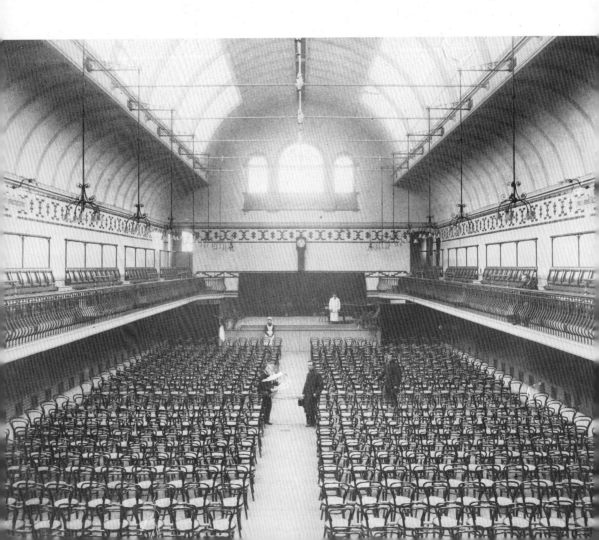

second rank'. Faint praise indeed for a man who came up with such a magnificent design. Now recognised as a Grade II listed building, it is officially described as 'constructed of red brick with Doulton terracotta bands and dressings' and as a 'large rectangular block in free Tudor/Francois Premier style' with 'steeply pitched slate roofs.'

The baths were opened by Alderman Sir Blundell Maple, who had made a fortune from his family's furniture store. 'Cleanliness is next to godliness,' Sir Blundell told the invited guests. It was his hope that children could be persuaded to use the baths. 'Get the little ones to be clean and they would be so through life.' With an orchestra playing a selection of Wagner, Strauss and Sousa, an aquatic display featuring 'ornamental swimming and motionless floating' by 'an expert troupe of ladies', diving and a water polo match, the baths were formally opened.

They featured four swimming pools: two each for men and women, divided into first and second class. The first class pools were larger than the second class and the signs for the men's pools can still be seen from Prince of Wales Road. The first class men's pool could be drained and the changing boxes removed so that events could be held in the winter months. It seated 450 people and was popular for concerts and film shows.

But the real benefit for the populace were the 129 'slipper' or washing baths for both classes and sexes. Here cleanliness was to be found and these went hand in hand with the public wash-house for clothes. This boasted fifty washing compartments, an ironing room with two mangles and a waiting room complete with a crèche supervised by a matron, who would look after the children while mothers were doing their laundry.

The baths remained open during the First World War. The building hosted a huge public meeting at which Ramsay MacDonald, later the leader of the Labour Party, was a speaker. During the Second World War water was needed to fight the fires caused by bombing and the baths were closed. When the war was over the baths re-opened and were modernised, not always very sensitively.

In October 2005 Camden Council considered closing the baths altogether, after a report described them as '100 years old and ageing', 'poorly designed' and 'at the end of their life'. Inclusion on English Heritage's Heritage 'At Risk' Register further highlighted the building's increasingly dishevelled state.

The Labour-run council baulked at the refurbishment which was estimated as costing up to £28.9 million. A passionate local campaign was launched and – after Labour lost the local ward election to the Liberal Democrats in May 2006 – the full refurbishment went ahead. The baths re-opened in July 2010 officially as Kentish Town Sports Centre, complete with a fully equipped gym. But to local people they remain 'the baths', and are as popular as they have ever been.

27 | FIND HOPE

Banksy chose the walls of Kentish Town and Camden Lock for some of his most memorable work. Acland Burghley alumnus Panik, aka Mr P, has populated our urban landscape with his trademark cross-eyed, square jawed characters and Elmo with slightly out-of-sorts monkeys. It's not quite Shoreditch, but NW5 and around has (or given its ephemeral nature, has had) some great street art.

But the most intriguing of this clandestine oeuvre is HOPE.

It's not really street art – but it's more than graffiti. The ten or so renditions of the word 'HOPE' – all in square-set capitals, in white paint, on rail bridges or close to rail lines – are as much a part of this patch as, well, Blustons or West Kentish Town station. Venerated by age, valued for bringing us a sense of the familiar – and a bit of a mystery as well.

Now, given the nature of the art not all that much is known about who painted HOPE, or why, or indeed when. Tentative enquiries to those in the street art scene have yielded no hard information. The general view is that these inscriptions are not tags but exhortations. This isn't someone marking their territory, but a plea, a prayer, an appeal to allow hope into our lives. The abundance of HOPE certainly suggests that whoever is responsible had a burning sense of mission.

Our favourite HOPE takes up the full width of the rail bridge across Athlone Street, just off Grafton Road – and that's the one that illustrates these pages. It's carefully executed, and embellished by those additional bits and bobs (known as serifs within the typographical trade) which make block capitals stand out. There are two other top notch renditions, again both on rail bridges. One is on Mansfield Road near Gospel Oak station, and the other at the south end of Kentish Town Road as you head out of NW5 towards the canal and our upstart younger sibling, Camden Town.

Then there's another batch of HOPE, not quite so imposing in execution, and without serifs, which nevertheless are recognisably of the same style and, we have to assume, purpose. There are (or were, one was painted over in early 2014) three close to the rail bridge over Highgate Road – then there's one alongside the pedestrian bridge over the rail lines at the side of Acland Burghley School – two a little out of our immediate area, on Midland Road near St Pancras station and on York Way – and the tenth has been all but scrubbed out, but if you peer hard you can see a faint trace of HOPE on the tallest part of Kentish Town station overlooking what some fondly imagine will be our Town square.

And the motive? God knows! Talking of which, it has been suggested that the Hope Chapel on Prince of Wales Road might be able to help with our enquiries. And enquiries have been made. Yes, they have clocked these inscriptions – no it wasn't their doing – but yes it is quite a pleasing hallmark of the area.

28 | PIANOS FOR ALL THE WORLD

On the tiny cul-de-sac of Perren Street, just off Prince of Wales Road, stands what was once an important part of the London piano and organ industry. Imperial Works was home to the Imperial Piano and Organ Company, exporting goods around the world.

The company was established in 1902 at Mare Street and Ellingford Road, but those Hackney premises were destroyed by fire in February 1919 and Imperial Piano moved to Kentish Town.

This is how Camden Council describes the building in its Conservation Area statement:

> The 'Imperial Works', a former organ works in Perren Street, is an attractive late Victorian building, in Gothic style, occupying the north west corner of the street. The façade has three gables with a varied outline, although upper and lower windows are generally aligned. The brick walls are patterned with dark red brick in polychromatic style and the wooden sash single bays and tripartite windows are set under segmental heads with keystone feature, also in dark red brick.

Sadly, the dark red bricks have been painted over.

Behind Imperial Works runs an alleyway, with steel tracks laid into the cobbles and complete with its own turning circle. Pianos and organs would have been lowered onto trolleys from the works above and rolled along to the northern end, where another alley joins Ryland Road. From there the goods could be transferred to carts or lorries for transport to their final destination.

Camden Town established itself as a major piano manufacturing centre in the nineteenth century, drawing industry away from Fitzrovia, because of the ease of transporting timber by canal, rail and road. It was said that every street in north London contained a piano works, and in many parts of Camden this was literally true. Between 1870 and 1914 Camden was the centre of the world's manufacture of pianos which were sent around the globe. There were around one-hundred in total. None now remain, although Heckscher & Company at 75 Bayham Street in Camden has been supplying piano parts since 1883 and still does.

The most magnificent piano warehouse is to be seen at 12 Oval Road. It is the circular building constructed for Collard & Collard in 1852. This building replaced a similarly shaped one, which was destroyed by fire a year after it was built.

With fifty-two bays, it was built around a central open well, to allow pianos to be hoisted from floor to floor during manufacture. The lowest floor was used for drying, the next for upright pianos, the second floor for cleaning, the third for polishing the cases and those above for 'belly' manufacture and finishing off. Collard & Collard were the oldest of the piano manufacturing firms of the St Pancras area, having patented a form of upright 'square' piano in 1811. Today their former manufactory houses offices.

29 | PROTECT AND SURVIVE

On Saturday, 7 September 1940, the Blitz began: 348 German bomb-ers and 617 fighters took part in the attack on London. The result was shocking: around 400 people died on the first day alone. Britain was poorly prepared, with few anti-aircraft guns and underpowered search-lights. The London Blitz was to last until 10 May 1941.

The Blitz sent Londoners scurrying for cover wherever they could find it; many seeking shelter in the Underground. These platforms and stairwells were often fetid, overcrowded and infested with lice, but they did become real communities. Swiss Cottage tube station even produced a newspaper – predictably called the *Swiss Cottager*!

The casualties would probably have been even heavier had it not been for a decision in 1938 to start providing individual shelters for families. Anderson shelters were named after Sir John Anderson, who had responsibility for preparing air raid precautions immediately prior to the outbreak of war. They consisted of two curved corrugated sheets of steel, bolted together at the top and sunk three feet into the ground then covered with eighteen inches of earth.

If these were constructed correctly, they could withstand the effects of a hundred-pound bomb falling six feet away. Even more importantly, they were to be put up in gardens, away from the falling masonry and beams that killed so many victims of the German attacks. The curved shape of the shelters allowed a bomb blast to travel around them, while the earth piled on top absorbed the shrapnel. They protected life from almost anything but a direct hit – as the remarkable picture from the Imperial War Museum, taken in Norwich in about 1941, shows.

The shelters measured 1.4 m wide, 2 m long and 1.8 m tall. They were quite cramped and anyone more than six feet tall would not have been able to stand up in one. Designed to sleep six people, they were not always popular with the public. Many Anderson shelters leaked and were chilly and dark. They also amplified the noise of falling bombs. It was difficult to persuade Londoners not to return to their warm houses as the weather got colder, despite the danger of being killed.

Anderson shelters were given free to all householders who earned less than £5 a week and those with a higher income were charged £7. Between February 1939 and the outbreak of the war, 1.5 million shelters of this type were distributed to the public. During the war a further 2.1 million were erected.

Many people who did not have one soon wished they did when the bombing began. This is the memory of Thomas Parkinson, of Kentish Town.

> We didn't have an Anderson shelter but there was one over the wall from our house. We had very heavy bombing one night and I climbed over the wall and cleared all the cats' mess out of the shelter and I went back to my house and went through the house telling everyone that the shelter was clear. By the time I went back to the shelter, it was full so I had to stand outside while they were dropping bombs at the end of the street.

The neighbourhood received its fair share of bombs, destroying many buildings. The shop front at Daniels, a shop then next to Blustons on Kentish Town Road, was hit. But by 1940 bomb damage had become

routine. A newsreel from that time showed some passers-by looking at the damaged window, whilst others walk past without bothering to take a glance. Among those who helped clear away Kentish Town's rubble was the renowned architectural historian, Nikolaus Pevsner.

Hitler had assumed he could break London's morale, but although the first four months of the Blitz had resulted in 22,000 deaths, this did not happen. The city continued to be attacked from time to time, with the VI and V2 rockets being used from 1944. The Anderson shelters had played a significant part in maintaining the city's morale.

After the war many of the shelters were dug up and destroyed. Households were supposed to return them to the local authorities to be smelted down. But some – including a few in Ryland Road, one of which is shown here – still remain, now serving as garden sheds.

30 | THE CRIMEA COMMEMORATED

Tucked away just west of the shop fronts and traffic of Kentish Town Road lies a network of small, rather charming streets. This is the Inkerman area, with many of the streets named after battles or generals from the Crimean War of October 1853 – February 1856. The houses, two or three storey buildings often with basements providing additional space, make ideal homes.

The Inkerman area is a thriving village. Its residents' association keeps a watchful eye on any developments and holds a popular summer festival, filling Alma Street and spilling out into Inkerman Road.

Many families are attracted to the area, and few leave; especially since the French School – or the Collège Français Bilingue de Londres, to give it its formal title – opened its classrooms in 2011. Taking over the old further education college on Holmes Road, the school has become a magnet for London's 300,000 – 400,000 French citizens. Today it is common to hear French in the pubs and cafés of Kentish Town.

Camden's conservation statement provides a neat description of the housing:

> *The Conservation Area contains a variety of small mid-Victorian two*
> *and three storey terraced houses built mostly within a decade in the*
> *1850s. All of the houses were built of London stock brick and most*

had stucco surrounds to windows and doors and other enrichments. Iron railings defined the front boundary of the small front gardens, many of which are now planted with shrubs . . . The houses were built incrementally, as the speculative builders' credit and cash flow allowed. Slight variations in architectural detail between groups of houses in the same street reflect the piecemeal process of development.

At the heart of the area is the Crimea pub. Once a favourite haunt of police from the Holmes Road police station, it is today divided into four flats. One of the residents described them as 'comfortable and spacious'. The pub sign still hangs outside.

Since most of the houses were built just after the Crimean War, it is not surprising that the names of the streets reflect this; whether there was a more personal link between the developers and the conflict is something of a mystery.

At the time, the Crimea was certainly very much part of British consciousness. The war was fought, as far as London was concerned, to prevent Russian expansion into the decaying Ottoman (or Turkish) empire. The Russians saw things very differently. They believed themselves to be the last outpost of the Orthodox Church following the capture of Constantinople in 1453. The Russian emperors felt they had a sacred mission to halt the Muslim hordes and protect the Christian faithful.

Whatever the cause, the war resulted in immense losses. More than half-a-million soldiers were killed in battle or died of disease. Britain alone lost about 20,000 troops.

Alma Street is named after the first major battle of the war, along the Alma river. The steep river banks were the last obstacle to the French, British and Ottoman advance on the city of Sevastopol. After fierce fighting, the river was crossed and the Russians routed, but at heavy cost. Legend has it that Manx soldiers were so moved by the battle that they made a pact to name all their first-born sons 'Alma'.

Having crossed the Alma, the allies were confronted by the Russians at the battle of Balaclava. Raglan Street commemorates Lord Raglan – the overall British commander. Lord Raglan is, perhaps unfairly, best known for a poorly worded order. It was his apparent decision to send the Light Brigade – the cream of the British cavalry – on a near suicidal mission to capture Russian guns for which he is remembered. His order despatched the 670 lancers into the 'valley of death', exposed to cannon fire from three sides. When they regrouped just 195 remained on horseback. The action was immortalised in the poem by Alfred, Lord Tennyson.

> *'Forward, the Light Brigade!'*
> *Was there a man dismay'd?*
> *Not tho' the soldiers knew*
> *Some one had blunder'd:*
> *Theirs not to make reply,*
> *Theirs not to reason why,*
> *Theirs but to do and die:*
> *Into the valley of Death*
> *Rode the six hundred.*

Modern historians believe the charge was not as futile as was first thought, but the suggestion that troops should succeed at any cost, literally 'do or die', was later interpreted as presaging the slaughter of the First World War.

After Balaclava the battle at Mount Inkerman, on the outskirts of Sevastopol, is recalled in the road's name. The fighting was again terrible and the British troops were being driven back when Major-General Sir George Cathcart (also remembered in a street name) arrived at the head of the 4th Division to plug holes in the British lines. Gathering around 400 men, Cathcart personally led an attack on the Russian flank, but was killed and his force broken up. The French had to come to the British troops' defence.

Willes Road received its name from Admiral Sir George Ommanney Willes, who took part in the bombardment of Odessa and of Fort Constantine at Sevastopol in 1854. For his services he was awarded the Crimean and Turkish medals, the clasp for Sevastopol, and the 5th class of the Mejidie and became a knight of the Legion of Honour.

The last street name to commemorate the Crimean war is Grafton Road, after the wonderfully named Lt.-Col. Augustus Charles Lennox FitzRoy, 7th Duke of Grafton. He fought in the Crimea, where he was severely wounded, and went on to serve as an equerry to Queen Victoria.

31 | BORIS THE CAT

Much missed by his owner, who commemorated his life with this memorial plaque at 24 Anglers Lane.

Passers-by remember Boris as a large, shaggy tabby, who was always in residence on the wall outside the house. He was beautiful and much admired, but beware petting him! His temper could be fierce and his claws raking.

Perhaps a typical Kentish Towner?

ACKNOWLEDGEMENTS

Of the archive pictures and illustrations included in this publication, that of Oswald Mosley on Islip Street is by courtesy of the Press Association; the still of the Kennistoun House rent strike is included with the permission of British Pathé; the portrait of Kwame Nkrumah is courtesy of Zuma Press; Fermin Rocker's painting 'Newspaper Kiosk, Tufnell Park' is included with Philip Rocker's permission; the wartime photograph of an Anderson shelter is from the Imperial War Museum; the photos of the baths on Prince of Wales Road are courtesy of Camden Local Studies and Archives Centre, Holborn Library; and the layout plan of the Camden Borough Control Centre appears on, and is published here with the permission of, the Subterranea Britannica website.

The map which graces this book was designed by Nancy Edwards whose website is at www.nancyedwards.co.uk

Tertia Nash and Sam White, design students at the University of Reading, gave *Curious Kentish Town* an ample dash of style and distinction – the authors are very grateful to them.

And we are also in the debt of all those who opened their doors, shared their stories, aided and abetted us in our endeavours, understood what we were up to, and helped make the compiling of this book such fun.

Five Leaves Publications
PO Box 8786, Nottingham NG1 9AW
www.fiveleaves.co.uk

www.curiouskentishtown.com

Text © Martin Plaut and Andrew Whitehead 2014

The moral rights of the authors have been asserted

First published 2014

ISBN 978 1 910170 06 9

Design by Tertia Nash and Sam White, students in the Department of Typography & Graphic Communication, University of Reading

Printed and bound in Great Britain